In The Shadow Of St. Patrick's: A Paper Read Before The Irish National Literary Society, April 27, 1893 : Containing Notices And Reminiscences Of Clarence Mangan [et Al.]

Patrick Joseph McCall

IN THE

SHADOW OF ST. PATRICK'S:

A PAPER

Read before the Irish National Literary Society,
April 27, 1893.

BY

P. J. McCALL.

CONTAINING

NOTICES AND REMINISCENCES

OF

CLARENCE MANGAN.	DR. WHALLEY.
FATHER MEEHAN.	ISAAC BUTLER.
O'CONNELL.	JOSUE JACOB.
ROBERT EMMET.	JOHNNY CREWE.
MAJOR SIRR.	"ZOZIMUS."
JEMMY O'BRIEN (the Informer).	KEARNEY THE SINGER.
SIR WM. PETTY.	DAN DONNELLY.
SIR TIM O'BRIEN.	JACK BOYLAN.

ETC.

DUBLIN:
SEALY, BRYERS & WALKER
(A. T. & C., L.),
94, 95 & 96 MIDDLE ABBEY STREET.

1894.

DUBLIN :
PRINTED BY SEALY, BRYERS & WALKER
(A. T. & C., L.)
94, 95 & 96 MIDDLE ABBEY STREET.

INTRODUCTION.

T HE manner in which the following little paper came to be written is simply told. When the Council of the Irish National Literary Society was preparing a series of House Lectures for the past Session (1893), it was remarked that none of the papers offered by the Members dealt with any special matter, being all of a general interest, broadly historical or minutely critical. Then it was suggested by the Vice-President (Dr. Sigerson), that some one of us acquainted with Dublin should endeavour to describe a particular locality of which he had some knowledge and in response to his invitation I undertook to

contribute some facts concerning the neighbourhood around St. Patrick's. The narration
may prove interesting, or it may not, but if
it should, I would feel encouraged to persevere
in the same direction with, perhaps, better
results.

In any case, I can fairly claim to have
collected a good deal of new matter, hitherto
unpublished, and in great danger of lying
for ever ungarnered.

IN THE SHADOW OF ST. PATRICK'S.

N considering the title of my paper, I find that I am precluded from dealing with a subject which at once forcibly attracts the attention, and this is, of course, the Cathedral itself. It is almost an act of self-denial to set oneself to the task of delving, as it were, amid the surroundings of such a stately historical old pile, remembering so many thrilling events connected with it, and to ignore, even then, its memories of Comyn and Marsh, of Swift and Vanessa, of James and William, to deal with events and personages possessing, by comparison, but trivial claims on our consideration.

But St. Patrick's, our pre-Union Valhalla, has already received full and competent treatment from many historians. The pages of Sir James Ware, Walter Harris, Messrs. Whitelaw, War-burton and Walsh, the unique MSS. of Butler and the ponderous tome of Monk Mason—all these afford such a mass of information regarding its foundation and its past and present glories, that I rather choose to put together a collection of notes relative to the neighbourhood and its people, very little of which has, as yet, been preserved within the safe and enduring pages of a book.

This task is still the more urgent, when I consider that a scheme for removing all the old landmarks is in a very forward state of completion. Already the process of dilapidation has developed to an alarming extent, so much so, that what a few years ago was a busy colony, full of recollections of eventful times and striking personalities, has already become like the ground covered by the palace of Aladdin, a waste of barrenness and desolation. Already I tremble to miss the haunts of Mangan and Tighe, of Lady Morgan and Sir Francis Burdett, of Swift and Petty, and a good many other folk who made a stir in Dublin life, long before the example of Haussman in Paris set civic authorities all over the kingdom full of enthusiasm to imitate on a small scale his colossal philistinism, in replacing every unique home of former times by the more sightly but scarcely more comfortable dwellings of *fin sièclism.*

St. Patrick's Cathedral is, as all Dubliners are aware, situated in the centre of the Liberties, and on the banks of the Poddle River.* By the way, I should like very much to have the derivation of this name satisfactorily explained. So far, I have never met with an explanation, and accordingly, without putting forward any pretentious claims, I beg to offer one. Some hold that it is a corruption of the word puddle, which by an easy process of transition, would become Poddle. But in my opinion this is not the case, and for this reason : The old inhabitants never say "The Poddle" but "*The Pottle*," and this, I think, affords a clue to its nomenclature.

We are told by Monk Mason and others that on the foundation of the Cathedral in 1170 by Archbishop Comyn, he granted to the chapter eight void spaces around it for the purpose of building residences for the clergy. These spaces around the church, then built on an island—it is called St. Patrick's *in insula* in the Bull of Pope Alexander III.—were afterwards known as the Liberty of St. Patrick's, and were invested with many privileges.†

---

* *The Poddle.*—This little river rises just at Tymon Castle in the Green Hills of Crumlin. It flows behind Mount Argus and Mount Jerome, and crosses under the canal near Richmond Bridewell. It is divided into two arteries at the Cross Poddle, now Dean Street, and joining again at the beginning of Patrick Street, it encircles the Castle of Dublin, and empties itself into the Liffey just under Duffy's the publishers, of Wellington Quay.

† *The Liberties of Dublin.*—These were districts originally outside the city proper, endowed with many privileges, and included the Liberties of St. Patrick's, the Liberties of St. Sepulchre, etc. The Earl of Meath's Liberty was

Now the word Pottle means a measure of land; so that the Pottle River is the river of the Liberty, or free grant. Dr. Joyce, in his *Irish Names of Places*, gives two names somewhat similar, and when he holds that Pottle Bane and Pottle Boy (both in the County Cavan) signify the white and yellow measure of land, I think my explanation at least worthy of attention and some consideration.

This Liberty, comprising the two Closes, was afterwards let on lease to various people, though at present there is but one ecclesiastical residence standing on it—that of the Dean. The Huguenots seem to have been especially favoured in being assigned plots; and the existence of a Sunday Bird Fair, in the North Close, still points to a former pursuit peculiar to the old French inhabitants.

Stranger still, this French colony at the beginning of this century, and more especially after the famine year, was ousted by a Gaelic one. Up to about five years ago the mellow accent of Munster and the shriller if more classical terms of Connacht might be heard just under the Cathedral in the locality named Walker's Alley

a later settlement of French Huguenots, mostly silk weavers. The Union put the *quietus* on this industry. There is a map of St. Patrick's Liberties given in Monk Mason's work at p. 10. An admeasurement made about 1750 gives 5 acres, 2 roods, 7 perches as its extent. Some of it was disputed ground between the Corporation and the Church authorities.

and Goodman's Lane—called after two aldermen of the Skinner's Row Corporation; but the houses are now levelled and their Gaelic inhabitants scattered.

Here to this Walker's Alley * came a County Clare tinker—one James Kearney, who settled there about fifty years since. Halliday Sparling, in his *Irish Minstrelsy*, says that he wrote many of the songs sung by Carey and other music-hall favourites, and that he died about twelve years ago. This first statement is not a fact, and though I rob a local celebrity of his laurels, I must in justice state that Kearney never wrote a line in his life, for he was hopelessly illiterate. I have a collection of about fifty songs bearing his name as author, but these were all purchased by him from others—all Liberty men, or natives of the district—from the witty Tom Shalvey, a gardener of the Tenters Fields; from John Doyle, a law clerk of Weavers' Square, and from Kane, a whip-maker of Cross Kevin Street—the usual price for each song being half-a-sovereign. But at least, as a wit and inimitable mimic, "The Raking Paudheen Rue," as Kearney called himself, is entitled to honourable mention.

Leaving these lanes, and going through another called Myler's Alley, formerly Glendalough Lane,

* *Walker's Alley.*—Another resident also famous in his day was Jack Boylan, the pugilist. A memoir of him has lately appeared in a Dublin paper. A local poet named Murphy also lived here, who used to talk in rhyme.

we pass under an arched house leading into Bride Street. On the right hand side is pointed out the cellar from which " The Nameless One "— James Clarence Mangan—was taken to die in the Meath Hospital. The cellar is filled in at the present time, and its entrance built up ; but remnants of the old trap door, the bulk head and balusters may still be seen. A little beyond it, at the other side of the street is the house, the Widow MacDonagh's,* Nos. 86 and 87, where the poet made his celebrated wager with Tighe, resulting in the remarkable elegy on the butcher, Johnny Kenchinow, of Patrick Street,† and which he read before the widow's comfortable taproom fire the very next evening, to Tighe's mingled surprise, delight, and mortification.

Facing it is a lane leading back to Patrick Street, where another butcher lived, who likewise received the honour of having an elegy written on him, but of a different nature from the fantastic rhyming one penned by Mangan. There have been worse things printed than this touching tribute to the memory of Thomas Kirwin of Bull Alley, written by his friend James Fleming, a

---

* *The Widow MacDonagh's*, now occupied by Mr. Andrew Cole. On Mrs. MacDonagh's death, about forty years ago, the house was rebuilt by Mr. Fortune of Grafton Street.

† *Johnny Kenchinow.*—His real name was Kinsella. The elegy is to be found in *The Life of James Clarence Mangan*, by John M'Call (my father), which can be procured at the *Nation* office, price threepence.

local bard, who has received a place in Mr. D. J. O'Donoghue's *Dictionary of Irish Poets.** Kirwan, who was a bit of a poet also, died in October, 1867 ; and from the elegy, written by Fleming, I give a few verses at random :—

October leaves
But thinly strewed the wooded hill,
And infant frost first kissed the rill,
When fell disease began to fill
The yawning graves !

.   .   .   .   .

Among the dead
My dearest friend, Tom Kirwan lies—
His witty puns and sharp replies
No more shall glad th' aspirant's eyes,
When they are read.

.   .   .   .

And we will weave
A garland of the fairest flowers,
That grow in Stella's † Sylvan bowers ;
And place it 'neath the ash that towers
Above his grave.

Here, also in this lane, lived Johnny Crewe, in his day the strongest man in Dublin. At the last riding of the Fringes, in 1839, this local Hercules went forth at the head of his butchers, and capturing the civic sword from its holders (the

* *James Fleming.*—Born in County Cavan, 1817, died at Great Strand Street, Dublin, January 12th, 1888. He was part editor of old Moore's Almanac (Nugent's), and wrote many songs, including " Mike of Mullaghmein," a '98 ballad. He was a daily visitant to the street until he got blind. His elegy on Thomas Kirwan appeared in the *Lady's and Farmers' Almanac* for 1868, published by Purdon of Bachelors' Walk.

† Swift's inamorata.

Ringsend sailors and Kevin's Port men) at Ball's Bridge, he held it in spite of all opposition till Clontarf was reached. Then, he obtained as his reward the release of a companion in durance vile for some transgression, and the Damon and Pythias of the Liberties were once more united in freedom and friendship.

But these are recent memories compared to those excited by the appearance of an old court in Bride Street, just opposite to Clarence Mangan's haunt (McDonagh's)—the court known still as "the Queen's Head." Here we come on the remains of one of our most famous hostelries, where we are informed by the late Rev. W. G. Carroll, Rector of Saint Bride's, in one of his many antiquarian articles, the mercurial Lady Morgan often put up in her visits to "dear, dirty Dublin." It is a pity that all this rev. gentleman's contributions on the antiquities of his parish (St. Bride's), lie buried in the files of old newspapers; for it is from recollection I am noting the fact I have mentioned. But, fortunately, I have happened on an account of the place, supposedly written by Dr. Burton, in a very whimsical and gossipy series of letters to an English friend, and published in a small volume entitled *Letters from Harold's Cross*, 1850. The copy which I possess has the rev. author's autograph. Here is what Dr. Burton says :— Dating his letter January 3rd, 1850, he thus

addresses a supposed English friend named
Wagstaffe :—

"It is now nearly thirty-three years since we
first met at Dempster's Old Queen's Head, in
Bride Street, where you had arrived from
England on a visit to the metropolis.

"Since that time the face of society has much
altered: that comfortable old hotel where we first
met, and in which Sir Francis Burdett put up on
his first arrival in this country, has now entirely
changed its character; 'tis no longer the Home
of the Traveller; yet, as I pass I cannot help
imparting to its dingy brick front the credit of
all the virtues that once reigned within.

"I am sure you recollect a broad old gentleman,
who was lodging there at the time of your visit
to this country. He was clad in a suit of honest
nappy black cloth of the period, strong silk
stockings and roomy shoes; his hat was high
and capacious. I remember he was in the room,
whilst we were at breakfast, and learning your
object, mentioned some of the places worth your
attention: amongst the rest, 'Aqueduct,' and
'Broadstone,' were impressed on my memory,
from the round and emphatic manner in which
he pronounced the words."

At the present day, this court, so dingy and
transfigured, would hardly pay the explorer in
search of old memorials for his toil and trouble;
but should he desire to see for himself what sort
these inns, such as the Queen's Head, were, in

the days of our grandfathers and great grandfathers, he can gratify his curiosity by examining
" the White Horse," in the Fire Brigade Station
in Winetavern Street, where the old inn still
remains in a good state of preservation.

Close by "the Queen's Head" is the old church
of Saint Bride's, where, for many years, the late
Rev. W. G. Carroll officiated. He has, as I have
said, collected a vast amount of information
regarding his church and parish, discovering a
mine of wealth in the old registers, dating back
to 1633, in excellent preservation—the most
valuable parochial collection in Ireland. Perhaps
the most remarkable personage connected with
this church was the notorious Sir William Petty,
who was a pew opener and vault owner here.
This man was an English tailor, who, coming
here to Ireland as an adventurer, became in the
end a millionaire, by methods, peculiar to the
times, such as the outlawry of native chiefs and
the confiscation and spoliation of their estates.
In addition to a Life of Petty in his pamphlet,
*The Landsdowne Irish Estates, and Sir Wm.
Petty*, the late incumbent gives a good deal of
information regarding other remarkable parish-
ioners, amongst whom were Sir William
Dunville; Colonel Hierome (or Jerome) Sankey,
a churchwarden also, and Petty's relentless
enemy; Major Ormsby, whose bowels were buried
in the cemetery, and for interring which, in 1663,
1s. 8d. was charged; Sir R. Newcomen; Mr.

Sands, also interred here ; Colonel Tomlinson, who prayed over the tailor millionaire, and Governor Hewson, who took a strange liking to the church and frequented it, in preference to all others—taking care, however, that there was a strong Cromwellian ministry maintained in it.

On the other side of the street is Chancery Lane, where O'Reilly's Irish Dictionary was printed, and where Clarence Mangan lived for years.* Mangan gives us a revolting and painful description of his home there, in his Autobiography —the outcome of a feverish diseased imagination, as unreliable as it is characteristic of the man and his awful moods of madness and depression. Further up, on the other side, at Derby Square,† is the house, where he went to school to Michael Courtney ; but fearing that I am going beyond "The Shadow," I will turn again to the west, and keeping outside the site of the city walls and the gate of Michael le Pole, I make my way back to Patrick Street.

Passing, then, from Bride Street through an alley—also called after the patroness of Ireland —I reach the Millyard, where once a mill on the Poddle flourished ; and, a little further on, I find myself at the spot once occupied by one of the

* *Chancery Lane.*—The Lord Chancellor's house is still standing—the remains of a magnificent building. It is next door to the police station, north side.

† *Derby Square.*—Opposite to this quadrangle is Hoey's Court, where Dean Swift was born.

gates of the city. This was St. Nicholas' Gate, at the junction of Nicholas Street and Patrick Street. Here there was a passage in the city wall (shown in Speed's Map, A.D. 1610), concerning which I get the following description* :—

" St. Nicholas' Gate have towe rounde towres without and sqware within, and the said gate placed betwixt both the towres, every towre three heights, whereof two lofts and foure lowpes in every towre : the wall five foot thick, thirty-nine foot in length one waye, and eighteen foot broad the other way, and the towre forty-five foot high, with a percullis for the same gate."

This gate, which was dismantled in the middle of the last century, held impaled on its summit the head of Luke O'Tuathail, of Castle Kevin, Lord of Fer Tire, County of Wicklow, and head of the Clan O'Tuathail (O'Toole). This prince levied troops in Leinster to defend Charles I. against the Puritans, and, falling into the hands of the Parliamentarians, was put to death by them, and his severed head exhibited over the City Gate.

Casting a glance up Nicholas Street, I will casually remark that in this street Edward Ledwich, the pseudo Irish antiquary, was born in 1739, and that a house, midway in it on the right, looking from the 'gate, was occupied by no less a personage than the celebrated Josue Jacob,*

---

* Gilbert, vol. i., page 185.

†*Josue Jacob.*—He lived at No. 34 Nicholas Street where he kept a tea shop until he became the Apostle and

"the White Quaker," whose doings and those of his spouse, Abigail Bale, would be well worth a chronicler's notice. The plot acquired for the interment of Josue Jacob and his sect is situated in Glasnevin Cemetery, on the walk leading from the graves of Terence Bellew MacManus, Leo, and Mahony, to the O'Connell Tower.

Returning to the site of the old gate, I find that the once famed Dr. Whalley, the notorious Quack, Star Gazer, and Almanac Compiler, was for a number of years an inhabitant of Patrick Street, occupying a house just outside the city (No. 1). Regarding the house on the opposite side, since pulled down to widen Blackhall Row, it was long a disputed point as to whether it was in the city or not, for, like the Gael who took a pledge not to drink inside or outside a public-house but stood on the threshold while so doing, this house was originally in the old wall, and consequently it was in a position similar to that of the imbibing Irishman. Even in recent years the parish priests of the two parishes used to claim dues from the owner—one because the man had his shop in the parish of St. Nicholas-within-the-Walls (St. Audœn's) and the other because he slept in St. Nicholas-without-the-Walls (*i.e.*, outside).

Founder of the Sect of White Quakers. Their tabernacle was in William Street and their convent at Clondalkin. Their nude procession from the latter to Holmes' Hotel (Ganly's) Usher's Quay, was one of the strangest sights of this century in Dublin.

B

But to return to Whalley. Gilbert says :—
" In 1709 we find Whalley exercising the trade
of printer and publisher, at the sign of the
' Blew Ball,' in Arundel Court, just outside St.
Nicholas' Gate, which barred the passage leading
from Patrick Street into Nicholas Street. Arundel
Court received its name from Robert Arundel,
who rented it from the Corporation, and a portion of it was covered over by the Blackhall
Row Market, so called after Sir Thomas Blackhall, who built it about the year 1783." It now
bears the name of St. Nicholas' Place.

This eccentric person, the " notorious John
Whalley," as Gilbert styles him, "the chief
quack and astrologer of his time," was a peculiar
character. Dr. Madden is more severe in his
terms, describing him as " the proprietor, editor,
and publisher of a newspaper, a quondam shoemaker, an astrologer, a quack doctor, an alma-
nack-maker, a no-Popery firebrand, a champion
of Protestant principles, and celebrated empiric
called Dr. Whalley."

We learn from himself that he was born April
29, 1653 ; but he does not tell the place of his
nativity. He is very exact as to the time and
situations of the heavenly bodies —"At 53 minutes
past 3 in the morning, Mercury being in Gemini,
gravidated by the friendly Sextile of Saturn
from Leo: the Moon in Libra, Jupiter in Aquary,
and both in trine to the Ascendant."

Originally an English shoemaker, about the

year 1682 he settled in Dublin, where he began
to compile his Prophetic Almanacs, after the
fashion of the English publications of the day,
and to practice medicine, with the usual specific
for all diseases, his "Golden Elixir!" He gained
such a reputation for necromancy that he was
even consulted by the authorities to discover for
them the whereabouts of the Duke of Monmouth.
He had his enemies, as the following rhyme
shows:—

> " Whalley, bred up to end and awl,
>   To work in garret or in stall,
>   Who had more skill in cutting leather
>   Than foretelling wind and weather,
>   Forsook the trade of mending shoes
>   To deal in Politics and News ;
>   Commenced Astrologer and Quack,
>   To raise the Devil in a crack ;
>   Told fortunes, and could cure all ills
>   With his elixirs and his pills.
>   Poor, petty servants, to their cost,
>   Flocked to him for all things they lost—
>   He pumped out all they had to say,
>   And getting all they had to pay,
>   The thief he showed them, in a glass ;
>   And, if she were a pretty lass,
>   He told her fortune must be great ;
>   If ugly, ah ! how hard her fate !
>   A hundred pretty things invented,
>   To send the wenches home contented."

In 1688, for his diatribes, the Roman Catholic
party being then in the ascendant in Dublin, he
was put in the pillory, and pelted with rotten

eggs ; and accordingly, during the Jacobite *regime*, he deemed it prudent to withdraw from Ireland. About this time, the Irish Bard, Feardaragh O'Daly, composed his celebrated satire on the astrologer, for which, in retaliation, Whalley caused the brother of the poet to be tried and hanged. In this satire—one of the bitterest in the Irish language, the poet first describes the wicked practices of the man, whom he declares to be in league with the devil, and who, since he began to view the moon and the planets, had with his basilisk eye destroyed their benign influence; so that the corn fields, the fruit trees, and the grass had ceased to grow, the birds had forgotten their songs, except the ominous birds of night—even the young of animals were destroyed in the womb. He then withers the astrologer with imprecations ; prays that all the diseases of earth may attend him ; and calls down on the impostor the curses of God, the saints, the angels, and all good men !

In England, Whalley kept a coffee house, and compiled two Annuals. *England's Mercury*, still preserved in the Bodleian Library, Oxford. Returning again to Ireland after the flight of James II., he lived for five years on St. Stephen's Green, at the sign of "The Blew Post," next door to "The Wheel of Fortune"—a very appropriate neighbour — finally removing to Arundel Court, off Patrick Street, where in 1714 he published a newspaper entitled, *Whalley's*

Newsletter. The supplement has been republished by Dr. Madden in his *Periodical Literature of Ireland.*

The incidents of Whalley's career, as compiled by Gilbert, Dr. Madden and John O'Donovan, are of so extraordinary a character, and so illustrative of the man and his credulous and superstitious times, that I know of no more interesting and engrossing study for an antiquarian enthusiast than is presented in the notices of him contributed by these eminent authorities. Whalley died at the good old age of 71, in the year 1724, " the year of darkness." Gilbert gives an epitaph which, he says, was written after Whalley's death, and which was widely circulated throughout the city. But here I feel obliged to correct even such a great authority as Mr. Gilbert on the correctness of his statement. Here is the alleged epitaph on Whalley :—

> " Here five feet deep, lies on his back,
> A cobbler, starmonger and quack,
> Who to the stars in pure good will,
> Does to his best look upward still.
> Weep all ye customers, who use
> His pills, his almanacs or shoes !
> And you, that did your fortune seek,
> Step to his grave but once a week :
> This earth which bears his body's print,
> You'll find has so much virtue in't,
> That I durst pawn my faith, 'twill tell
> Whate'er concerns you just as well,
> In Physic, Stolen Goods, or Love,
> As he himself could when above !"

The above epitaph was never written on Whalley, but was composed by Dean Swift, of St. Patrick's, on the demise of another impostor and quack named Partridge. Partridge died in 1708, or sixteen years before Whalley; but the terms, applicable to the one seem so very appropriate indeed for the other, that possibly, the epitaph may have been used for both. But Dr. Madden gives an epitaph, composed on Whalley by a humorist, whom he calls "the facetious Jemmy Carson," but it is of too coarse a nature to bear quotation.

In after years this house (Whalley's) was converted into an inn, which, at the beginning of the century, was owned by the popular Sir Timothy O'Brien. The worthy baronet appears to have been an eccentric character in his way, and among a certain class of his customers (before he resigned his retail for a wholesale store) he was invariably known as " The Knight of the Battered Naggin," recalling Cervantes' Knight of the Golden Basin in *Don Quixote*. This cognomen of Sir Tim had reference to the dilapidated conditions of his pewter measures, by means of which, his customers asserted, the niggard landlord saved a goodly amount of the precious liquor. Still, in spite of that drawback, they continued to patronise his establishment, allured, perhaps, by the enticing fact that it contained home manufacture in the shape of potteen. For the production of this, Sir Tim had special facilities; for underneath his cellar ran the little river Poddle, which crosses the street at this place, and into which all the surplus matter connected with distillation could be safely let flow.

Sir Tim, having been elected a Member of the Dublin Corporation, in course of time was chosen Lord Mayor. In this capacity he had the good fortune to receive the Queen on the occasion of her visit to Ireland in 1849. As the story goes it is asserted that on his presenting the keys of the city to her at Baggot Street, her Majesty was inclined to confer the honour of knighthood on her watchful officer; but he refused it at the time, to receive later on the more dignified and higher grade of baronetcy.

In Glasnevin Cemetery, not far from the graves of Denis Florence MacCarthy and Doctor Denis Phelan, and next to that of the faithful and patriotic William Fitzpatrick, one of O'Connell's bailsmen at the time of his prosecution, this remarkable, self-made man is interred. His monument is a very imposing structure, and is situated on the left of the walk as you go from the O'Connell Tower to the old entrance, and quite close to the site of the former mortuary church. In addition to being Lord Mayor, Sir Timothy O'Brien occupied a seat in Parliament, as, later on, did his kinsman, Sir Patrick, Member for the King's County in Butt's Party.

Sir Tim was succeeded by a strange character named Curran, nicknamed " Corny," and regarding him and his house, I have been fortunate enough to meet with a notice which I shall submit later on.

A little further down in Patrick Street, on the opposite side, and at the corner of Bull Alley (formerly Bride's Market) there lived another almanac compiler, a pupil of Whalley's, named Isaac Butler.   In the *Irish Builder* for May, 1889, I find an account of him, showing him to be a man of even more ability than his master, or at least one who turned his knowledge to better account.

This Isaac Butler was employed by the Physico-Historical Society of 1744, to make inquiries after rare plants, fossils, simples, and such like curiosities, as enumerated in their proposals for that year.   He was also instructed to draw up lists of all the indigenous plants then to be found in the neighbourhood of Dublin, with their names and localities ; and while so engaged, Dr. Rutty employed him to procure specimens of mineral waters.   The Dean and Chapter of St. Patrick's set him to work to gather materials for a history of the Cathedral, and the result of his investigations is now to be found in a small quarto MSS. book deposited in their archives.   This MSS. book was well known to Monk Mason, the historian, for he gives several extracts from it in his work.

It is not known the year in which Isaac Butler

was born;* but he died December 7th, 1755, as we find from an entry in the minutes of the Medico-Philosophical Society for that year. The minute is well worth reproduction :—

"On Tuesday last, at 7 minutes, 4 seconds past 3, Post Meridian descended to the Antipodes or Nadir (the Lower Regions?) at his lodgings, under the sign Leo in Taurus, or Bull Alley, Dublin (corner of Patrick Street) the Umbra or Penumbra of Mr. Isaac Butler, Ptolmean Philomath, Judicial Astrologer, Discoverer of Losses, Botanist, and Calculator of Nativities, having passed the meridian of life and his grand climacteric, in the 66th year of his age. He had formerly been a student under, and for several revolutions of the globe was successor to, the late truly great adept. Dr. John Whalley, Professor of the celebrated Astrological Art of the Doctors Lilly and Partridge of Bickerstaffian memory,—which Dr. Whalley did, for many years, calculate and publish the principal almanacs in Ireland, at a time when judicial astrology was held by philosophers in such reverence that they thought it rather a supernatural gift than a science, founded on sidereal influences. The like learned Ephemeris and Predictions, since his master's culmination in the *Medium Cœli* below the horizon, have been annually set forth by Isaac Butler, who was a kind of Gymnosophist and Rosicrucian, well skilled in the occult sciences and all the wisdom of Ptolomy, Erra Pater, Cornelius, Agrippa, and Tycho Brae, which besides the changes which were to happen in our atmosphere and other—the usual furniture of Kalendars—contained the Geocentric Courses, Revolutions of Aspects of the Planets, calculated for the meridian of this Honourable City of

* *Isaac Butler.*—He was born, I find, in 1689. At the time of his residence at the corner of Bull Alley he had for a neighbour a Counsellor Mitchel—two doors away was the well-known "Butchers' Arms."

Dublin.   He also inherited from his master many physical secrets, and gained such a knowledge in Botany, that he not only collected simples for the curious and officinals for the sick, but he also taught several tyroes in Pharmacy to know most of our indigenous vegetables.   December 7th, 1755, this truly great adept departed this life, having hastened his end, by laudanum taken in brandy, which he prescribed for himself, in order to die like Socrates and other antient sages."

In spite of this flattering testimonial to Butler's skill in predicting events, which are supposed to cast their shadows before, I find an amusing circumstance recorded which is rather calculated to throw some doubt on his ability as a prophet, however much he may have excelled as a Gymnosophist or a Rosicrucian.

Like master, like man.   Dr. Whalley had a rival named Coats who gave him much trouble; and in the same way our prophet Butler had an antagonist named La Boissiere, who published an opposition almanac every year.   As two of a trade can never agree, so in the case of the two Dublin seers, the adage was verified to the fullest extent.

In one of his Almanacs entitled, " A Voice from the Stars, for 1727," Butler took the trouble of erecting " A Scheme of the Heavens " to suit the supposed time of his rival La Boissiere's birth.   From the positions of the planets thereon he foretold a series of evils and misfortunes for his rival, who would, on a certain day named, miserably end his life.   But Butler caught a

Tartar on this occasion. In spite of the fatal prediction, La Boissiere survived, and, to make matters worse, Butler's own father, when walking through the streets on that ominous week, was killed by a vehicle! As everything is fair in war time, this sad event gave La Boissiere an opening to cast ridicule on his antagonist's skill as a prophet. "Why," said La Boissiere, "did not this competent prophet, who is able (according to his own account) to prognosticate all the vicissitudes of life that mortal should go through —why did he not set himself to read his own father's horoscope, and, from a foreknowledge of the impending fate that awaited him, have *kept him at home* on that unlucky day, March 5th?" Evidently La Boissiere scored a point in his retort, but it was somewhat uncharitable to have seized hold of such a sad calamity for securing a victory.

Very nearly opposite, at No. 16, is the house where that eccentric individual, Michael Moran, better known as Zozimus, lived for years, and where he died on the Friday before Palm Sunday, 1846. From a rather scarce little book, published by Gill, we learn that he was born in 1794, at Faddle Alley, off Black Pitts, at the other side of the Cathedral—a locality which, it has been said more than once, "has more pigs than Protestants." But as this book, in my opinion, is very apocryphal and unauthentic in some parts, I shall not intrude on the preserve, but shall supplement it, by some excerpts which I have taken—one from the *Shamrock*, written twenty years ago, by M'Cormack, a bookseller on Wood Quay, and the other from a chapbook, published by Harding, of Werburgh Street in this vicinity—a printer, who shares with the well-known Nugent the work of providing our street and village vocalists with much of their pabulum.   Mr. M'Cormack, in the course of his business as a bookseller, happened on an old Dublin newspaper, in which were reported the proceedings of the Henry Street Police Office.   One of the cases before the magistrate was a charge against Michael Moran for "obstruction and annoyance," caused by singing songs in the public streets.   The offence took place in that classic locality known as Cole's Lane Market, off Great Britain Street; and on the hearing of the case, a sympathetic recording angel being present, we have the following report handed down to posterity :—

Magistrate—"What have you got to say to this charge ?"

Zozimus—" Your worship, I love me counthry. She's dear to me heart, an' am I to be prevented from writin' songs in her honour, like Tommy Moore, Walter Scott an' Horace done for theirs, or from singin' them like the an-shent bards, on'y I haven't got me harp like them to accompany me aspirations !"

Magistrate—" But you are not to collect

crowds around you, so as to obstruct the public pathway, and prevent the people from passing."

Zozimus—"That what I sing is the praises ov me native land ; an' the highways shall sound with the voice of pathriotism. The Repale cry has gone forth, like the wings ov the mornin, (to borry a metaphor from an author I admire) ; the magic ov the sound has penethrated into every hovel, an' the people stand forth in their might. The mighty laider, great in his power, an' secure in the justice ov his cause, has pro- claimed the triumph ov Freedom, an' the nation has responded to his call. Why, then, should I be idle ? ' To him that much is given, much will be expected.' An' as a portion ov the poetic janius ov me counthry has descended upon me showlders, ragged an' wretched as the garmint that covers them, yet the cloth ov the prophet has not aroused more prophetic sintiments than I entertain, that me counthry shall *be* a free counthry ! It is thrue I can't see ; but I can warble that which can rise the hearts ov me counthrymen ; an' if crowds gother 'round me how can *I* help it ?) Homer sung the praises ov his counthry on the public highways ; an' we are in- formed that dramatic performances wor performed in the streets, with nothin' else for a stage but a dust cart. (Laughter.)) Ah, gintlemin, ((*aside*— Good Chrest'yans, are their worships list'nin' to me ?)—if me productions contain an'thin' that's thraisonable you can punish me ; but first hear me before you judge ! "

Then Zozimus repeated the following lines :—

" Though my coat is all tore, me muse is yet young,
   Though the cowld dhrops ov winther me body may wet;
Yet Lord Ebrington's speech hasn't dried up me tongue,
   So I'll sing for an' shout out for Liberty yet ! ·

The aigle ov Liberty flocks round our isle ;
   An' brave Connemara's sons hail the bright day—
The lasses ov Limerick lend their fair smile,
   An' laid us to battle—hurray, boys, hurray !

The thistle ov Scotia may flourish in pride ;
   But can they forget the dark day ov Glencoe ?
The rose ov proud England may bloom be its side,
   An' boast ov the glory ov famed Waterloo.

But the meek little Shamrogue of Air'yun's fair land,
   Is fifty times fairer than any ov those ;
An' the Temperance Movement, so morally grand,
   Will laid us to glory without any blows !

Then hurray for Repale ! for rivers an' strames
   Can turn all the wheels ov the mills in the wurrld ?
Our thoughts through aich day, an' at night, our sweet
     drames,
   Shall be for Repale, an' its bright flag unfurled !

Oh, Air'yun ! the land ov bog, mountain an' glen,
   Arise in thy might, like a lion at bay ;
For we're eight millions ov stout sober men,
   To repale the curst Union—hurray, boys, hurray ! "

The magistrate could do no less than dismiss the case, cautioning Zozimus against obstructing the thoroughfare in future, in which case he would be punished severely.

My next notice of Zozimus is taken from one of Harding's song books, and in which another character equally well known in Patrick Street as "The Sugar Cane," is introduced. I have condensed the original sketch very much, but have added a great deal of information to it, which only a person well acquainted with the neighbourhood would be able to supply.

The writer of the sketch in Harding's book, when a little boy, was sent by his aunt to purchase a ballad from Zoz; and for this purpose he had to intercept the old man when coming from the Smithfield Market, one of the poet's haunts. The minstrel's way would lead him to cross the bridge into Winetavern Street, and up St. Michael's Hill to Nicholas Street; and so, at the corner of Christchurch Place the youngster took his stand. At this place of junction he noticed a large crowd around a little handsome man, with a drab coat and white apron, who, with a tray suspended by a strap before him, dilated on the advantages of his "Sugar Cane." This, a species of sweetmeat, was laid out in symmetrical rows, while, in prose and verse, the vendor recited its magical properties, interrupting a most exalted discourse on occasions by such remarks as:—

"Take your hand off ov the tray, boy—go to school!" or

" Plaze make room for the lady to pass in!"

Among other advantages, the little man attributed to the constant use of his sugar cane the pleasant expression to be seen on every true Irishman's face, impervious even to the saddening influence of a bailiff in his house ; and he instanced the case of Dan Donnelly, the prize fighter, in his combat with Cooper, regarding which we have a multitude of Dublin street songs extant.* According to the Sugar Cane Man, the immortal Dan was being worsted in that fierce fight on the Curragh till Miss Kelly (Lady Captain Kelly *recte*), who had everything she possessed in the world staked on her champion, waved her hand at him, and with a bewitching smile gave him a packet containing two ounces of the cane, whispering :—

> " Now my charmer
> Give him a warmer !"

" The result," said the little man, "is a matter of history "—at which statement there was great commotion amongst the knights of the steel and

---

* *Daniel Donnelly.*—I have three songs in my collection penned in praise of the Irish fistic champion, beginning severally thus :—

" You songsters all rejoice, with a united voice
    While we support the choice of Ireland's present pride."
            — *Verses in praise of our Irish champion.*

" Ye muses I beg you will lend me your aid,
    Till I sing of brave Donnelly, a true Irish blade !"
            — *Donnelly and Olliver.*

" You lovers of the manly art of self-defence attend,
    I'll sing for you a verse or two that lately I have penned,
    Concerning Daniel Danley, that Irishman so bold,
    Who fought for Erin, and his country never sold !"
            — *Lines written on Donnelly the Irish champion.*

cleaver, or, as they have often been called, " The Bull Alley Yeomen," by whom Dan Donnelly was revered as a demi-god. This is not to be wondered at ; for the great fistic champion was, as it were, one of themselves, and for a long time kept a public-house on the Cross Poddle,* at the corner of the New Row and the Coombe, a little south-west of the Cathedral. Prior to that time he had been living nearly opposite, at the corner of Francis Street.

Taking advantage of the opening in the crowd to let "the lady" pass in, the writer went in search of Zoz, to whom he was well known as the little boy who often led him across the streets and saved him from the rush of the cattle on market days. Meeting the old man coming up " The Hill,"† the boy delivered his message, and the two proceeded down to Patrick Street as far as Corny Curran's—the house occupied in former years, first by Whalley, and then by Sir Tim O'Brien. Having entered, Zoz, feeling fatigued after his climb, made inquiries from " Masther Mike Slattery," Curran's assistant, concerning some "whiskey droppings" kept for him, and having imbibed to his heart's content, he proceeded to his home in Cole Alley. Here, in company with such well known " Liberty Birds" as "Peg the Man," " Stoney Pockets,"‡ "Dandy-

---

* Now Dean Street.
† St. Michael's Hill.
‡ Mentioned in Patrick Kennedy's "Banks of the Boro."

orum," and "Fat Mary," celebrated in Kearney's songs, the poet lived occasionally, though his usual abode was in Patrick Street, at Nos. 23 and 16.

Reaching the second floor and raising the latch, the following amusing colloquy occurred :—

" Where a' ye, Johnny ? "

" Under de table, daddy ! "

" An' where's your mammy ? "

" Gone to de fountain wid de taypot ! '"

" Gone to the fountain with th' taypot ?—ah, just as Masther Mike said : ' Moran, it's all the fault of your taypot ! ' " (Zoz had been complaining of the poor quality of Curran's tea to Mike).

" Mary, dear," said the poet, when his wife entered, " I'm distressed to think that the charakter of Masther Mike's Bohay should suffer through an unscientific application on your part ! " and with this introduction, he launched out into an exhortation on the baneful effects of using a cold teapot, concluding with a receipt, after the manner of Carolan, in the following lines :—

> " The proper way
> To make your tea
> Is, when your water's boiled,
> Take your pot,
> An' make it hot,
> If not, the tea'll be spoiled ! "

The lecture on tea-making being over, he proceeded :

" Mary, dear, this boy here has a message from Miss W—ll, of Back Lane—the lady I meet comin' from the 12 o'clock Mass in Adam and Eve's—God bless her!" (Adam and Eve's, the familiar name for the Franciscan church on Merchants' Quay, and one of the few churches, if not the only one, accorded the privilege of having the celebration of Mass at noon on week days). " She's wantin' ' Billy's Downfall ' for a friend who is leavin' town this evenin'."

" Sol Kelly" (another ballad singer), said Mrs. Moran, " got the last one in the place."

"Indeed!—Johnny," (this to his son) "go down stairs an' tell Sol Kelly I want him."

After a few minutes Sol Kelly made his appearance—a diminutive man with a Jewish countenance.

" Good mornin', Mick," said he, " what soort ov a market had ya?"

(" I thank you for the inquiry Sol," said the poet—" grandly appreciative—the ethereal thunder of Dan's eloquence in Mahony's last week, has greatly affected the market for the betther. It has entered the souls of the men and stirred the pockets of the women. Ah, Sol, when I come to the ind of the third verse:—

> ' O'Gorman Mahon will back brave Dan,
>   We care not for the College, O.'

the air becomes balmy with the sighs of sweet defiance, and I can hear the *rhinos* in the pockets of the crowd strugglin' for freedom, to exacute a transmissive gallop.")

Here a rap at the door announced that Sol was wanted in all haste.

"Before ye go, Sol," said Mick, "I want the ballid of 'Billy's Downfall' you got from Mary: it was the on'y one left."

"Oh, I have it safe, Mick," said Sol; "but the last four lines of the third verse can't be read, the prent is so bad!"

"The third verse," said Mick, "that's the Johnny McCrea verse: but if ye send up a pen an' ink, Sol, the young lad here will be good enough to write down the four lines."

After a graceful apology from the poet for the delay occasioned by the typographer's remissness, he proceeded to recite the four lines of the ballad, which deals with an attempt to blow up the statue of King William III. at College Green :—

"I care not for no man, High Dutch or Low man;
With watchmen when tipsy, I might have a brawl;
But by all the old stitches in Johnny's old breeches,
I ne'er had a hand in King Billy's downfall!"

The Johnny alluded to is, of course, Johnny McCrea, the tailor of Dawson Street, and a leader in the old Tory Corporation.*

Regarding Zozimus' "Mary dear," we learn that she was his second wife—a widow named Curran, or, as his biographer quaintly puts it :—

* *Vide* the old Dublin street ballad, "Bishop McCue and the Pedlar," to the air of "Derry Down!"

" Twice did he venture into the chariot of Venus by doing the connubial ;" while little Johnny, who was amusing himself *under de table* on the occasion of our chronicler's visit, we are told, grew up an intelligent boy. In after years, a sea captain, who lived at Eldon Terrace, Clanbrassil Street, took a liking to him and brought him to sea on several voyages. Johnny afterwards settled in New York, and to this place his mother and a stepsister afterwards emigrated. The death and burial of Zozimus is fully described in his life, and this portion of the biogram is really authentic. He died at 16 Patrick Street, and is buried at Glasnevin. Should any admirer wish to locate his mound, he will find that it is situated in the poor ground A. G. 30, south ; there is, or used to be, a red ash on the right-hand side, two feet, from the head of his grave.

In the account which Zoz gave his bosom friend, Sol Kelly, of the state of the ballad market, he made allusion to the " ethereal thunder of Dan's eloquence at Mahony's last week," as affecting the market for the better. This, of course, refers to O'Connell, and to one of his many speeches at Mahony's Great Rooms, now occupied by the houses Nos. 24 and 25 Patrick Street. And, by the way, Zozimus himself lived for years in a small back cottage, now dismantled, at the rere of 23. This was previous to his later residence in Cole Alley, or to his last one at No. 16.

These two houses, enumerated above, have a special and historical attraction. At the beginning of the century, they were occupied by a man named M'Gauran, whose people afterwards owned a large establishment in Westland Row, at the corner of Lincoln Place. At the rere was a large dyer's, and the store there was rented in 1803 by a Scotchman named M'Intosh (who is described as being then forty years of age) on behalf of Robert Emmet, to be used as a depot for rockets and grenades, and for the manufacture of powder. Associated with M'Intosh were Michael M'Daniel a dyer by trade (and thus possessed of some chemical knowledge), two assistants named Keenan, and a tailor named Kirwan, of Plunkett Street, a few hundred yards distant.

By some means or other, M'Daniel, while making rockets, let a spark fall on some gunpowder, and an explosion took place. This soon brought Major Sirr on the spot, who arrested a number of people, among whom were M'Gauran, the proprietor of the front house. Dr. Madden has unearthed a report from the *London Chronicle* of October 8, 1803, which states that M'Intosh made an important statement to Sheriff Pounden,* in consequence of which Major Sirr repaired to M'Intosh's residence, where he dis-

---

* *M'Intosh.*—See Dr. Madden's *Lives,* vol. iii., p. 360. M'Intosh can hardly have been an informer, as he was executed for his connection with the explosion.

covered a concealed door, artfully formed of bricks, built in a frame, plastered over to resemble the adjoining wall, that was covered with shelves and turned out upon hinges and castors. Upon opening this door a tier of closet rooms appeared, communicating by trap doors and scaling ladders through the different storeys of the house. These rooms were spacious enough to contain forty men, and were provided with air holes opening to the outer wall.

After a search the Major discovered from 300 to 400 pikes of a peculiar construction, having an iron hinge at about half their length, by which they doubled up, and though, when extended, they were six feet long, yet by this contrivance it was possible to carry one of them under a man's coat. A quantity of sulphur was likewise found, and every appearance of much more serious preparations having gone forward in the house.

Major Sirr brought away the door as a curiosity, and for a long time it remained in his office in the Castle.

Regarding the fate of the men found on the premises, we learn, from the Dublin papers of the 4th October, 1803, that John M'Intosh, lately convicted of high treason, was executed in Patrick Street, opposite the depot of which he had charge, and shortly after M'Daniel, the two Keenans and Owen Kirwan suffered the same fate. A remarkable story is told of one of the Keenans.

With the rope around his neck, about to be hanged, he saw before him in the crowd his own wife, holding her children by the hands. Her pitiful appeals for mercy were, of course, disregarded. In vain she appealed to them not to take away her only support, until at last, finding that they would wait no longer, her husband, taking up the coat which he had discarded, threw it to her, saying, " Here, Mary, take this —it'll get you at least one meal for the children !"

Another man who suffered death on this occasion was a silkweaver named Valentine, of Plunkett Street, then a busy hive of the silken industry. On hearing the report he concluded that it was the signal for the insurrection, and, putting on his uniform—being a man of means—he sallied out into the streets, to fall into the hands of the authorities. I heard this incident from an old man named Tierney, who died a good many years ago at an advanced age. That the Valentine family lived in the street is proved by the following epigram in the *Budget*, July 17, 1832 :—

" ON THE MARRIAGE OF MISS VALENTINE, PATRICK STREET, TO MR. W——, OF GRAFTON STREET.

" In times of old, young folks were gay—
In spring they kept up Valentine's Day ;
But now 'tis changed, I can't tell why—
Some get their Valentines in July !"

As to M'Gauran, who was also arrested, we

find the following information in Dr. Madden's book, which, by the way, is very confused and contradictory in many parts. He says :—" In turning their prisoners to pecuniary account Sirr and Sandys played into one another's hands. The Major made the arrests, turned over the prisoners to Sandys and O'Brien (Jemmy the Informer),* and the latter duly worked upon their hopes and fears, alternately threatening

* *Jemmy O'Brien, the Informer.*—I have picked up the following remnant of a Dublin street ballad concerning this well-hated individual :—

> " Jemmy O'Brien, he was the boy
> That would patriots destroy ;
> And if he wouldn't take them up,
> He'd finish them like Hoey !
> With his dagger
> How he'd swagger,
> So furious and so eager !
> And so ruthlessly, too, would he slaughter
> The husband, the wife, and the daughter—
> Your favourite, great Jemmy O'Brien ! "

Then Jemmy is made to say :—

> . . . . . .
>
> " A croppy I secretly made him,
> Then I as quickly betrayed him,
> In the bastiles so quickly I laid him ;
> Likewise the brave Arthur O'Connor,
> He was fired at by Jemmy O'Brien."

> . . . . .
>
> " The braggart he now is pulled down,
> And all the great lawyers of the Crown
> Could not save poor Jemmy O'Brien ! "

them with perpetual imprisonment, transportation, or the triangle, and acquainting them with the kindness of the Major's heart, the forgiveness of his disposition, and the necessity of making a proper compliment, either in goods or money.

"Every act of favour or indulgence was a perquisite in the provost. Heavey's liberation cost him a mare (about which there is a comic song extant); M'Gauran's (of Patrick Street) cost him a house in Tallaght. This man was nowise connected with Emmet or cognisant of his plans, but he had a quantity of wine, strongly suspected of being long in bottle. He was arrested by the Major, sent to the Provost, and committed to Sandys, he came out deprived of nearly all his property."[*]

There can be no doubt but that the premature explosion in Patrick Street interfered very much with Emmet's plans. It is said that he was even in the place at the time, and that he and Michael Dwyer paid it and the other depots daily visits. Dr. Burton, who gives very many interesting particulars regarding the insurrection and capture of Emmet, says, that whenever he (Emmet) ventured into town, he crossed over the garden ground, where Heytesbury and New Bride Streets now stand, and confined himself principally to

---

[*] *M'Daniell.*—A family of this name lived early in the century at No. 16, the house in which Zozimus afterwards died.

the obscure streets about Saint Patrick's, dining in the eating houses which then abounded there, and where he met his friends.

On M'Gauran giving up the place the Mahony family acquired the two houses, and on the death of the owner, Alexander Mahony,* his widow still continued to carry on the hotel. "Mahony's Great Rooms" soon became renowned all over the city. Here were accustomed to assemble all the politicians of the day, and many an election speech was delivered by O'Connell and Ruthven, Parliamentary candidates for the City of Dublin, from its windows. A Repeal reading-rooms was started here, and the

---

* *Emmet's Arsenal.*—Dr. Madden in a note makes the misleading statement that the house where the explosion took place was situated opposite the Cathedral, and he describes some house there, probably 36. How he makes this mistake I cannot imagine. The number of the house behind which the explosion took place as given in the Dublin papers of the day is 26, and that the numbers of the houses have not been altered since, is proved conclusively by reference to the old leases of the church property, where the numbers exactly correspond to those at present in existence. In a MSS. book of subscribers' names to the Roomkeepers' Society, Mr. Thomas M'Gauran is given as living in 24 Patrick Street in 1808, when the book begins. The house visited by Dr. Madden had, however, unknown to him, an interesting history also attached to it. During the "Riding of the Fringes" this house, 36, being alone on that side in being a Church Liberty, had to be encircled by the Lord Mayor and his procession, but part of its yard being municipal property was crossed. Probably Dr. Madden was misled by the owner's name M'Gowan, it being very like the other's (M'Gauran) and imagined he was a descendant and living in the old house.

large hall at the rere used for political dinners and meetings. As O'Connell never omitted making a speech on such occasions, the multitude outside would wait patiently, amusing themselves with bonfires made from elm trees stolen from the canal between Clanbrassil Street Bridge and Parnell Bridge, till, dinner being over, he would appear at one of the front windows to commence his address.

Perhaps his most momentous visit was in 1842, when, dressed in his mayoral robes and wearing the collar of SS., he attended the annual dinner of the Malachian Orphanage, an institution still in existence on Arran Quay. His visit is thus described by the author of *The Liberator, His Life and Times* :—

" A few days after (his inauguration) O'Connell attended the dinner of Saint Malachi's Orphan Society. With his usual felicity of expression, he referred to the splendid gold chain of the Corporation, which he wore, saying :—

" ' I am here, it is true, but an uncanonised Malachi; I resemble the old monarch of that name, of whom the poet sings :—

" Malachi wore a collar of gold ! "

" ' He won it, we are told, by the same authority, " from the proud invader "; whereas, I won *this* from the old rotten Corporation of Dublin ! ' "

Among those who dined here with O'Connell was the late Father Meehan of loving memory. I have heard him tell that the first public dinner at which he attended, when a young curate, was at these rooms; and one day, he spent a long time going about the place, trying to recal its former appearance; but it was all changed   At last, he noticed, with peculiar satisfaction, a large beam which stretched across the entire floor, for he at once remembered, that it was under it he sat, on that memorable day of old.   It would afford me much gratification to recount many other things concerning the house (for I live in it) —of the pottheen making of McGauran, who made use of the Poddle river over which the house is built—of all the great dinners and re-markable demonstrations told in later years to me, by " Katty Crick " (*cruit*, a hump) and Anne Bates, known in the neighbourhood as O'Connell's cooks, and of many other strange doings, but I must not omit including their favourite recital :— How, one day, O'Connell being more than usual well pleased with the entertainment provided, or perhaps with the state of the Repeal Exchequer, would not depart till he had first seen and thanked his " little cooks," as he called them. And, " Oh, think of me and Anne," said Katty, " to be brought up to the great man and to be patted on the head, and we in our white bibs, after gettin' ready the dinner ! "   This incident I know, was a memory green in their souls, till death took them both.

On Mrs. Mahony's retiring from business in 1848, the large hall was demolished by the landlord, who holding different political opinions, declared that never again would he have such people as the Repealers meeting in his house. The establishment was then divided into three, the spacious rooms narrowed, the large hall thrown down, and the space it occupied converted into three back yards. This state of things still continues.

I have purposely avoided all notice of the street during the Fenian uprising, for the time is not yet opportune for so doing; but I may remark that the contingent supplied from the neighbourhood included the bulk of its inhabitants, and that many of the houses are associated with the names of Fenian generals, colonels, captains, and even a paymaster.

I have now arrived again at Saint Patrick's Cathedral, when I find that I cannot restrain from adding a few notes concerning its chequered history. Recently, on an old book stand, I came across a small book, bound in the Irish blue, and bearing on its cover a gilt impression of the Cathedral as viewed from the west, and having the Gaelic title of "Ceallphort Naoimh Padruig, le Eilis O'Domhnaill." I thought I had hit on a history in Gaelic of the old pile, but to my chagrin I found that the title was the only Irish words in the book; however, the patriotism of the authoress is to be commended. The history of the Cathedral may thus be briefly summed up: Built by Archbishop Comyn, on the site of an old church erected (according to Jocelyn, an uncertain authority) by Saint Patrick, it underwent many changes in course of time.

In 1541 the Houses of Parliament met there to confer the title of King of Ireland on Henry VIII. who returned the compliment when he changed his religious opinions in after years, by destroying most of the building and many of its sculptures. Edward VI. turned it into a law courts and grammar school, and Cromwell used it as a barracks for his soldiers. James II. restored it to the Roman Catholics, and William III. upset this arrangement and transformed it into a Protestant Cathedral; this it has remained. ever since.

Its monuments at present are numerous and interesting, and amongst them, those erected to the memory of Swift, Stella, Schomberg; the Boyles, Earls of Cork; Captain Boyd; Curran, Balfe, and Carolan, the last of the harpers, are perhaps the most conspicuous.

With this notice I conclude my paper. It is true, and I regret it, that many things which I have given are but of local interest, and may not be attractive for the general reader. This could hardly have been avoided, hemmed in as I was by the very title of my paper; but as life is made up of trifles and matter of atoms, so History consists of the record of local events, such as mine, from which, choosing the most remarkable, the historian, manipulating the mass, produces that monument which every nation should and ought to possess—a history of its people, for the people—a work of which we in Ireland are sadly in need, and for which we are so long and anxiously awaiting.

Printed by SEALY, BRYERS & WALKER (A. T. & C. L.), Dublin.

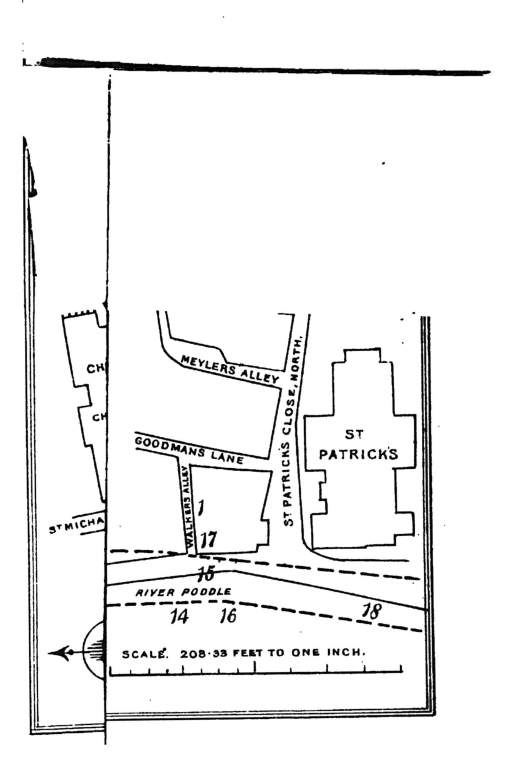

MEYLERS ALLEY

ST PATRICK'S CLOSE, NORTH.

ST
PATRICK'S

GOODMANS LANE

WALKERS ALLEY

CH

CH

ST MICHA

ST MICHA

1

17

15

RIVER PODDLE

14   16   18

SCALE. 208·33 FEET TO ONE INCH.

that monument which every nation should and
~~ought to possess—a history of its people, for the~~